D1163144

CALVIN HILL

AND

GRANT HILL

ONE FAMILY'S LEGACY IN FOOTBALL AND BASKETBALL

Jason Porterfield

rosen publishing's
rosen central

New York

Published in 2010 by The Rosen Publishing Group, Inc.
29 East 21st Street, New York, NY 10010

Library of Congress Cataloging-in-Publication Data

Porterfield, Jason.
Calvin Hill and Grant Hill: one family's legacy in football and basketball / Jason Porterfield.—1st ed.
p. cm.—(Sports families)
Includes bibliographical references and index.
ISBN 978-1-4358-3549-8 (library binding)
ISBN 978-1-4358-8516-5 (pbk)
ISBN 978-1-4358-8517-2 (6 pack)
1. Athletes—United States—Biography—Juvenile literature. 2. Hill, Calvin, 1947–Juvenile literature 3. Football players—United States—Biography—Juvenile literature. 4. Hill, Grant—Juvenile literature. 5. Basketball players—United States—Biography—Juvenile literature. 6. Fathers and sons—United States—Juvenile literature. I. Title.
GV697.A1.P578 2010
796.092—dc22
[B]

2009023683

Manufactured in the United States of America

CPSIA Compliance Information: Batch #LW10YA: For Further Information contact Rosen Publishing, New York, New York at 1-800-237-9932

On the cover: *Left:* Dallas Cowboys running back Calvin Hill drives downfield during Super Bowl VI, played in 1972 against the Miami Dolphins. The Cowboys won 24–3, earning the team's first Super Bowl title. *Right:* Detroit Pistons forward Grant Hill finds an open lane and drives inside during a 1995 game against the Chicago Bulls. Though only in his rookie season, he was already emerging as a major star.

On the back cover: NASCAR is a registered trademark of the National Association for Stock Car Auto Racing, Inc.

Contents

Duke Blue Devils players Grant Hill and Christian Laettner high-five each other during the NCAA championship game against Kansas in 1991. The two teammates were instrumental in helping Duke win the NCAA championship.

The Duke University Blue Devils were ahead

5–1 during the opening minutes of the 1991 National Collegiate Athletic Association (NCAA) men's college basketball tournaments championship game against the University of Kansas Jayhawks. Duke guard Bobby Hurley lobbed a pass to forward Grant Hill, who was near the basket. The pass went high, but Hill made a spectacular leap, grabbed the ball one-handed, and slammed it through the basket to score.

The play was the game-defining moment for Duke, as the Blue Devils went on to win the tournament. It was also a sign of great things to come for Grant Hill, who became one of the National Basketball Association's (NBA's) biggest stars.

Hill's father, Calvin Hill, watched the play from the stands. More than 20 years earlier, he had been a football standout at Yale University before becoming a star halfback and running back for the National Football League's (NFL's) Dallas Cowboys.

Together, Grant and Calvin Hill represent one of the strongest and most unique family legacies in professional sports. Both had outstanding college careers and later were chosen in the first round of the professional draft for their respective sports. They were each honored with awards for their achievements as rookie players and went on to set milestones for their teams.

Calvin and Grant Hill gained the respect of their teammates and opponents on the football field or the basketball court. Both also looked beyond their sports. For Calvin, that meant raising Grant to be competitive and mentoring him through the early years of his own career. For Grant, it meant growing up to become the type of player whom his father could admire and respect.

Chapter One

EARLY YEARS

Calvin Hill and his son, Grant, grew up in radically different times and circumstances, but both were taught to work hard and excel at whatever they did. Calvin's father, a construction worker who never graduated from high school, encouraged him to do well in sports and apply himself to his studies. After Calvin became a celebrated professional football player, he would credit his father for teaching him to work hard.

When his son, Grant, was growing up, Calvin and his wife, Janet, worked to teach Grant to push himself and compete at a high level. They also taught him to be humble and give back to the community.

YOUNG CALVIN HILL

Calvin Hill was born on January 2, 1947, in Baltimore, Maryland. He grew up in nearby Turner's Station, Maryland. When Calvin was young, his father encouraged him to participate in Little League sports, and he played both baseball and basketball.

When Calvin was 14 years old, he won a scholarship from a local doctor to attend the Riverdale Country School, a private high school in New York City. He continued to play basketball, averaging 20 rebounds per game in his junior and senior years, and once scoring 56 points in a single game. Calvin also began playing football for the first time. He blossomed into a four-sport star as he continued to play baseball and participate in track and field.

Calvin Hill was a multisport star throughout his high school and college careers. Here, he is shown competing for the Yale track team in the broad jump in a 1967 meet.

FOOTBALL SUCCESS

Calvin excelled at football, making the varsity team in his freshman year and growing into his role as the team's quarterback. During the four years that he attended Riverdale, the football team had a 51-game winning streak. In his senior year in high school, Calvin was named to *Parade* magazine's All-America football team.

The All-America honors and his status as an honors student at Riverdale brought many college recruiters out to meet Calvin. He was approached by schools with big football programs, as well as by Ivy League schools like Yale and Harvard.

Though he was interested in playing college football, Calvin didn't seriously consider playing football professionally or which school would give him the best chance to make it to the NFL. Instead, he was planning to attend divinity school after graduating from college. He would later say that he had one main priority at the time for evaluating college football programs: he wanted to play for a team with a big football stadium where he could compete in front of huge crowds.

An assistant football coach at Riverdale encouraged him to consider the Ivy League schools Princeton, Harvard, Dartmouth, and Yale. The coach, a Yale graduate, arranged for Calvin to visit the school in New Haven, Connecticut. The

Calvin Hill reaches for a pass from Yale quarterback Brian Dowling during a 1967 game against Penn State.

JANET HILL

Calvin Hill met Janet McDonald at a party after a football game in 1968. They got married in 1970. McDonald attended Wellesley College and was in the same graduating class as Hillary Rodham Clinton, who later became First Lady, a U.S. senator, and secretary of state. As Calvin Hill continued his football career, McDonald earned a master's degree in mathematics education at the University of Chicago, and she worked as a teacher, a special assistant to the secretary of the U.S. Army, and a researcher for a private consulting firm.

McDonald had a clear idea of how she wanted their son, Grant, to grow up. She raised him to be polite and disciplined. He and his friends sometimes called her "the general" because of all the rules that she made him follow. Even today, Grant credits his mother for giving him his sense of self-discipline by teaching him to follow rules and put others before himself.

weekend that Calvin visited Yale also happened to be the weekend of a big football game against Dartmouth. Yale's football stadium was filled with about 63,000 avid fans that watched the game. The game-day excitement thrilled Calvin. He decided to apply to the school, and he was later accepted.

YOUNG GRANT HILL

Grant Hill was born on December 5, 1972, in Dallas, Texas. At the time, Calvin was playing professional football for the Dallas Cowboys. In 1976, the Hills moved to Reston, Virginia, a suburb of Washington, D.C., when Calvin started playing for the Washington Redskins. The Redskins' practice facility was

Calvin and Janet Hill celebrate Christmas with a very young Grant Hill in 1973. Calvin's arm is in a sling after he dislocated his elbow during a late-season game.

located near the Hills' home, and Calvin would often bring his friends from the team over to his house after practice.

Calvin and his wife, Janet, encouraged Grant to play sports. Grant began playing soccer when he was just five years old. Two years later, he started playing basketball. But, at first, he did not like the sport as much as he liked soccer. Grant's soccer team won a youth league state championship twice.

One sport that Grant did not play was football. His parents told him that they would not let him play football until he was in high school. One reason was the fear of injury. Calvin had been injured many times during his football career, and the Hills worried that Grant would damage his still-growing body while playing football.

They also worried about stress. Calvin thought that if Grant started playing football, he would always be pressured by coaches to be as good at the sport as his father. Calvin also worried that such pressure would be bad for Grant's self-esteem. Instead, Grant devoted himself to playing basketball and soccer. By the time Grant was old enough for his parents to let him play football, he had lost interest in the sport.

FINDING BASKETBALL

Grant's interest in basketball grew steadily. Calvin often played one-on-one games with his son, and they started going to college basketball tournaments together. When Grant was in the seventh grade, he made it onto a traveling Amateur Athletic Union (AAU) basketball team called the Northern Virginia Hawks. In 1985, just before Grant entered the eighth grade, his team won a national tournament.

Soon after the win, Grant stopped playing soccer and began concentrating on basketball. In 1986, he played in another national AAU tournament and was named its Most Valuable Player (MVP).

When Grant entered the ninth grade at South Lakes High School, the time came for him to try out for basketball. He was expected to play on the junior varsity team with his friends. But the varsity coach knew about his skills and asked him to try out for the varsity team.

At first, Grant refused to do so. He didn't want his friends to think that he was better than they were. He also thought that his father had influenced the coach. Calvin had to convince Grant that he had earned the tryout based on his own merit. He made the team and became the first freshman ever to start on the team. He also led his AAU team to another championship and was named tournament MVP for the second straight year.

Throughout his son's high school career, Calvin continued to encourage him. He watched Grant's games closely. At the end of each game, he would talk with Grant about how the game went, pointing out what his son had done well and what he needed to work on. Calvin would also evaluate Grant's playing at the end of the season. During high school, Grant played at both guard and forward.

Grant averaged 25 points per game in his sophomore year. As a junior, he broke his high school's career scoring record. He was named the Northern Virginia Player of the Year three times and made *Parade* magazine's All-America team as a senior. At the end of his senior season, Grant was chosen to play on an All-Star team of players from across the country. The team competed in the Junior Championship of the Americas and won a gold medal for 1989–1990.

When the time came for Grant to choose a college to attend, his parents recommended two different schools. His mother wanted Grant to go to Georgetown University in Washington, D.C. His father wanted him to attend the University of North Carolina, the school of basketball legend Michael Jordan. Instead, Grant chose to enroll at Duke University in Durham, North Carolina.

Chapter Two

COLLEGE CAREERS

When Calvin went away to college at Yale, he had little idea of what to expect. Although his parents supported him in playing football and earning his degree, neither of them had ever been to college and thus had no firsthand experiences to share.

Grant, however, was the child of two college graduates. Calvin and Janet both had high expectations for him. They recognized that basketball would be a major part of his life at Duke, but they wanted him to really apply himself to his studies and earn his college degree. Calvin had already experienced life as a college sports star at Yale and worked to help Grant adjust to playing basketball at Duke.

CALVIN HILL AT YALE

Calvin earned a football and track scholarship to Yale through his hard work at Riverdale. Yale has long been considered one of the most elite colleges in the United States. Yale also has a proud football legacy and devoted fan base, as Calvin learned when he first visited the school and saw the Bulldogs play Dartmouth.

Calvin wanted to earn a place in Yale history by becoming the Bulldogs' first African American quarterback, the position he played in high school. During his second day of practice with the team, however, he was shifted to linebacker. In high school, Calvin had been at the center of every game.

While Calvin Hill sometimes became discouraged during his freshman season on Yale's football team, he stayed with the program and became one of the team's leading scorers and biggest stars.

At Yale, he didn't even get to play in his first four games. He felt so discouraged that he considered quitting the team.

He finally got to start at fullback in his fifth game. Calvin quickly adapted to his new role on the team, using his speed and agility to become one of the team's leading scorers. During the four years he played at Yale, he ran for 24 touchdowns and passed for another 6. He led the team in touchdowns with 7 and rushing yards with 463 in 1967, and again with 680 yards and 14 touchdowns in 1968.

THE YALE VS. HARVARD TIE

When the Yale Bulldogs played against their archrivals, the Harvard Crimson, near the end of the 1968 season, both football teams were undefeated. Yale was expected to win over the relatively inexperienced Crimson.

At first, the game went as expected. Yale running back Calvin Hill rushed for one touchdown, which broke the school's old scoring record. Yale held a 29–13 lead until the game's final four minutes, when the upstart Harvard team scrambled to score 16 more points. The game ended in a 29–29 tie, and the two teams shared the Ivy League title with identical 8–0–1 records. However, many shocked Yale players and fans who had expected the Bulldogs to win, including Hill, considered the tied game a loss.

BREAKING RECORDS

In 1968, Calvin scored 13 touchdowns in games against Ivy League opponents, tying the Ivy League record and setting a Yale team record that stood until 2006. He set another team record against Ivy League schools by scoring 78 points that season. And his six touchdown receptions in 1968 still rank him number 10 on Yale's all-time list. Calvin's average of 22.2 yards per catch in 1968 is still a school record, as is his career average of 18.8 yards per catch.

In 1967 and 1968, Calvin helped lead Yale to Ivy League championships as the school went undefeated in both seasons. He was selected to the conference's All Ivy first team both seasons and was named to *Parade* magazine's All-America football team in 1968. That season, Yale's football program also honored Calvin by giving him the Chester J. LaRoche Award. The award is given to the senior player who, by his character, academic talents,

The Dallas Cowboys chose Calvin Hill in the first round of the 1968 NFL draft, following his record-setting career at Yale. Calvin's hard work and leadership also earned him the respect of his teammates and classmates.

and concern for others, does the most for Yale. Calvin was the award's first recipient. His teammates also honored him by presenting him with the Jordan Olivar Award, which is given to the senior player other than the team captain who, through his devotion to football, earns the highest respect of his teammates.

THE NFL DRAFT

Despite all of his success on the field and the honors he had earned, Calvin still did not seriously consider playing professional football. He expected to graduate with a degree in history and then attend divinity school. However, his success on the football field and the honors he earned in his final season made him a nationally known player. When he decided to enter the 1969 NFL draft, he was picked in the first round—24th overall—by the Dallas Cowboys. After meeting with legendary Cowboys coach Tom Landry, Calvin decided to put graduate school on hold. He signed a contract to play professional football with the Cowboys.

GRANT HILL AT DUKE

Grant knew at a young age that college coaches wanted him to play for them. He received his first recruitment letter when he was just a sophomore in high school. Hundreds more would come in the years that followed.

Grant chose Duke partly as a compromise between his parents' wishes, but the school's excellent basketball program was a deciding factor. Although the Duke Blue Devils had never won the NCAA basketball tournament, the team had advanced to the tournament's semifinal Final Four round eight times and played in the championship game in 1990, the year he graduated from high school. Grant was impressed with Duke's basketball coach Mike Krzyzewski, who told him during a campus visit that he would have to earn a starting place on the team. Other coaches that Grant had met had promised him that he would start as a freshman.

Calvin supported his son's decision to go to Duke University. He and Janet met with Krzyzewski and liked the way that he ran his team. Krzyzewski had a code of conduct for his players to follow and knew how to get the most out of them without resorting to threats or intimidation.

Even though he had always followed the rules that his parents set out for him when he was in high school, Grant sometimes quietly rebelled against Calvin. During his football career, Calvin had always taken pregame preparation seriously. He believed he had to be in the right frame of mind in order to play well. He would eat the same meals and spend the

Calvin Hill watches Grant and the Duke Blue Devils defeat the Purdue Boilermakers during a 1994 NCAA Tournament game. Calvin attended many of his son's games during Grant's time at Duke.

same amount of time relaxing and focusing before going to the field hours in advance to prepare for games.

Although Grant worked hard at basketball, he never established a pre-game ritual while he was in high school. Calvin pushed him to focus before games, and Grant understood how important these preparations were to his father. Grant was so successful on the court and his high school team was so good that he didn't feel the need to spend the extra time focusing before games. In his 1996 memoir, *Change the Game*, Grant explained that by not establishing a pregame routine, he was trying to set himself apart from his father.

ARRIVING AT DUKE

When Grant got to Duke University, however, he had to change his habits and spend more time practicing and preparing. He often called his father when he felt discouraged. Calvin would reassure Grant and give him advice on staying focused. Calvin also attended as many Duke home games as he could. He was a constant presence in the stands behind the Duke bench.

The Blue Devils started the season ranked among the top 25 college teams in the country. Grant was one of the youngest players on the team. Much of the attention was focused on the team's stars Christian Laettner and Bobby Hurley. Although Grant was happy to let other players lead the team, his father and Coach Krzyzewski encouraged him to step forward and become a star. While he was far from the team leader, Grant managed to score 10 or more points in each of his first six college games. He played well for the rest of the season and was named a Freshman All-American and was picked for the Atlantic Coast Conference's (ACC's) All-Freshman Team.

As it became obvious that Grant had great talent on the court, he started to receive more attention from the media. During his high school career, local reporters had often interviewed Grant. Many would ask him about being Calvin's son, or even interview Calvin and write about Grant in their stories. However, during Grant's time at Duke, reporters started

Grant Hill passes around Kansas Jayhawks player Alonzo Jamison during the 1991 NCAA championship.

interviewing Calvin. Although they would sometimes ask him about a particular game, they would also ask him about being Grant's father. Fortunately, Calvin enjoyed talking about his suddenly famous son.

Duke earned a place among the 64 teams in the NCAA tournament that season and went on to win its first national championship that year by beating the University of Kansas Jayhawks. Grant played well as a forward during the tournament and, at age 18, became the youngest player ever to start in a Final Four game.

A SECOND CHAMPIONSHIP

When the season ended, Calvin praised his son for his skill on the court. He also suggested that Grant work on improving his defense. Grant took his father's advice to heart and became one of Duke's best all-around players the next season. When teammate Bobby Hurley became injured and had to miss several games, Grant took over his position as point guard and adjusted well.

Later in the season, Grant also became injured. By the time he was fit to return, Duke was already playing in the ACC tournament. Calvin had taught him the importance of making sacrifices for the team, and Grant understood that returning to the starting rotation during the tournament could upset the team's chemistry. He gracefully accepted that he would play from the bench, but he started during the NCAA tournament. Duke

The Duke Blue Devils and head coach Mike Krzyzewski celebrate the team's victory over the University of Michigan Wolverines in the 1992 NCAA championship game. Grant Hill is shown at the far left.

won the championship again in 1992 by beating the University of Michigan Wolverines. They became the first team to win back-to-back championships since the 1970s.

After the 1992 tournament win, Duke star Christian Laettner graduated. Grant emerged as one of the team's leaders for the 1992–1993 season. He averaged 20 points per game early in the season, but he broke several bones in his foot during a game in late January and had to stay off the court for six months.

This was Grant's first major injury of his career. Calvin, who had dealt with many injuries during his career, advised Grant to be patient and let the injury heal. Grant took his father's advice and used the time off to reenergize.

The next season, Grant was the team's clear leader. Few people expected Duke to advance far in the NCAA tournament. Grant, however, predicted that the team would make it to the championship game. He led Duke to a 24–8 record and to the championship game, where the Blue Devils lost to the University of Arkansas Razorbacks by a score of 76–72.

At the end of the 1993–1994 season, Grant was named the ACC's Player of the Year, as well as a First-Team All-American. He finished his career as the first player in the Atlantic Coast Conference to collect more than 1,900 points, 700 rebounds, 400 assists, 200 steals, and 100 blocked shots in his career. He also became the eighth Duke basketball player to have his jersey retired.

Shortly after graduating from Duke with a degree in history, Grant entered the NBA draft and was picked in the first round, third overall, by the Detroit Pistons. Like his father, Grant would compete in the world of professional sports.

Chapter Three

GOING PRO

Although they played different sports in different eras, Calvin and Grant Hill both made a huge impact during their careers. Calvin became one of the NFL's top running backs during a time when it was still uncommon to rush for more than 1,000 yards in a season. Grant was often heralded as one of the most complete players in the NBA and basketball's next superstar. Both father and son battled potentially career-ending injuries, but returned to contribute to the success of their teams.

CALVIN HILL IN THE NFL

When the Dallas Cowboys picked Calvin in the first round of the 1969 NFL draft, some Cowboys fans were unhappy with the choice. Calvin had a great career at Yale and had been named an All-American, but Yale was not a school that produced many professional stars. As though he had some doubts himself, Calvin enrolled in graduate studies at Southern Methodist University and took classes in the academic discipline of divinity while playing for the Cowboys.

ROOKIE SEASON

Calvin soon silenced the unhappy Cowboys fans with his competitiveness and excellent play. By the fourth game of the 1969 season, Dallas coach

Calvin Hill won over many fans and earned the NFL's Offensive Rookie of the Year award during the 1969 season. In this photo, he is driving downfield in a preseason game against the San Francisco 49ers.

Tom Landry was calling him one of the best players that he had ever seen. The Cowboys finished first in their division with a 11–2–1 record, and Calvin was a key contributor to the team. He finished the season with 8 touchdowns and rushed for 942 yards, nearly becoming the first rookie to rush for 1,000 yards. For his accomplishments, Calvin was named the NFL's Offensive Rookie of the Year, made the league's All-Pro team, and played in the Pro Bowl.

Calvin showed Cowboys fans that he belonged on the team in his rookie season. The next two seasons were disappointing, as injuries cut into his playing time. Calvin started the 1970 season by rushing 577 yards for 4 touchdowns, but a leg injury kept him off the field for the team's final games and appearance in Super Bowl V. It was the Cowboys' first Super Bowl, and they lost to the Baltimore Colts, 16–13.

Calvin also lost playing time in 1971, as his leg continued to heal. He returned to play in 8 games, rushing for 468 yards and 8 touchdowns and catching passes for another 3 touchdowns. Another late-season injury limited his time in the playoffs as the Cowboys advanced to the Super Bowl again, and he was not able to start in their Super Bowl victory over the Miami Dolphins.

As the 1972 season started, Calvin was determined to make up for the time he had lost in the previous two seasons. By the end of the season, he was once again recognized as one of the league's best runners. He rushed for 1,036 yards,

THE WORLD FOOTBALL LEAGUE

The World Football League was founded in 1974, with 13 teams based in cities across the United States. Some of those teams, like the Honolulu-based Hawaiians, were the first professional teams in their cities. The teams attracted NFL stars by promising high salaries and the chance to be a part of something new.

As the 1974 season got under way, the league looked to be a huge hit. Attendance was high, and the league's founders discussed expanding it into Europe and Asia. However, many of its teams soon encountered financial problems. The World Football League folded in 1975 after only one full season.

becoming the first Dallas player to rush for more than 1,000 in a season, and led the Cowboys to the playoffs. He scored six touchdowns rushing, another three receiving, and played in his second Pro Bowl.

Calvin topped his 1972 rushing total by rushing for 1,142 yards and 6 touchdowns in the next year, the third most in the league. The Cowboys made their eighth consecutive playoff appearance, and Calvin made the Pro Bowl again. His numbers fell in 1974, as he rushed for 844 yards and 7 touchdowns, but he still made his third consecutive Pro Bowl.

LEAVING DALLAS

The year 1974 was Calvin's final one with the Cowboys. He left the team at the end of the season and joined the Honolulu-based Hawaiians of the World Football League, a league that hoped to bring football to the global stage. When the league folded the next year, Calvin returned to the NFL

Late in his career with the Cleveland Browns, Calvin Hill leaps over a Chicago Bears player to avoid a tackle during a 1980 game. Calvin was known throughout his career for his speed and athleticism.

with the Washington Redskins. Injuries from previous seasons had started to slow him down, and he had to play as a reserve. Though the Hills had moved to Washington, D.C., so that Calvin could be near his family during the playing season, he left the Redskins after the 1977 season.

Calvin planned to retire from football when he left the Redskins. As time passed, he found that he still wanted to play, so he joined the Cleveland Browns. Although he started some games with the Browns, Calvin was again mostly used as a reserve. Still, he helped the Browns make the play-offs in 1980 before retiring for good in 1981.

GRANT HILL IN THE NBA

Thanks to three appearances with Duke University in the NCAA championship game, Grant was already a well-known sports figure when he started his first season in the NBA. In 1994, the Detroit Pistons were recovering from a series of losing seasons. Head coach Don Chaney saw Grant as the type of player that he could build his team around.

ROOKIE OF THE YEAR

Grant had a remarkable rookie season with the Pistons in 1995–1996. He became very popular through his easy charm and skill on the court. When the time came for basketball fans to select the NBA All-Star team, Grant received more than 1.2 million votes—more than any other player in the league. He was the first NBA rookie ever to lead the All-Star balloting.

On the court, Grant lived up to his reputation as a complete player. During his rookie season, he averaged 19.9 points, 6.4 rebounds, 5.0 assists, and 1.8 steals per game. He lead the team with 1,394 points that season, becoming the first Pistons rookie since Isaiah Thomas in 1981–1982 to score more than 1,000 points.

The Pistons ended the season with a losing record, but Grant was named the NBA's co-Rookie of the Year, sharing the award with Jason Kidd of the Dallas Mavericks. Winning the award meant that Grant had matched one of his father's accomplishments. Although Calvin and Janet had raised their son to be humble, Calvin had also encouraged Grant to be very competitive, even in the one-on-one basketball games that they had played when Grant was growing up. By winning the award, Grant was able to keep pace with the extraordinary beginning of Calvin's NFL career.

Grant Hill *(left)* shared the 1995 NBA Rookie of the Year award with Jason Kidd of the Dallas Mavericks. Grant was proud of matching his father's NFL Rookie of the Year Award.

PLAYOFF RUNS

Grant played forward for the Pistons for six seasons, emerging as the team's leader. During those years, he led the team to four playoff appearances and was named to the All-Star team six times. He was chosen to play on the 1996 U.S. Olympic basketball team, helping the team win the gold medal. At the end of the 1998–1999 season, Grant became only the second player, along with NBA legend Wilt Chamberlain, to lead his team in scoring, assists, and rebounds in a single season three times.

Grant had his best year as a scorer in 1999–2000, when he finished third in the league with 25.8 points per game. The Pistons made it to the playoffs again, losing to the Miami Heat. In the final weeks of the regular season, Grant injured his left ankle. He decided to play in the playoffs anyway, which only made the injury worse. He was again chosen to be on the U.S. basketball team for the 2000 Olympics, but he had to turn the offer down because of his injury.

Grant Hill passes the ball during a 1999 game against the Denver Nuggets. This was Grant's best season as a scorer.

INJURY PROBLEMS

Before the start of the 2000–2001 season, the Pistons traded Grant to the Orlando Magic. Grant hoped he could lead his new team to the playoff success that he didn't experience with Detroit. However, his injured ankle kept him off the court for all but four games in 2000–2001. The next three seasons were no better. He played in only 14 games in 2001–2002 and just 29 games in 2002–2003.

The injury was severe enough that it almost ended Grant's career. It also nearly cost him his life. After undergoing surgery on the ankle in 2003, he developed a serious staph infection and was hospitalized. After having surgery to repair the damage, Grant ended up missing the entire 2003–2004 season.

Grant returned to form in 2004–2005, playing in his first full season since leaving Detroit. He averaged 19.4 points per game and was voted an All-Star for the first time since the 1999–2000 season. Though injuries kept him off the court again for most of the 2005–2006 season, Grant helped the Magic reach the playoffs in 2006–2007.

At the end of the season, Grant left Orlando and joined the Phoenix Suns, helping the Suns reach the playoffs in 2007–2008 and rejoining the team for the 2008–2009 season. "I'm just amazed by him," Suns head coach Alvin Gentry said of Grant after a 2009 game against the Utah Jazz, according to Hill's official Web site. "He's just a big-time competitor and such a smart player."

Chapter Four

LIFE AND LEGACY IN SPORTS

Calvin Hill retired from football in 1981. Although his son, Grant Hill, was one of the NBA's biggest stars during the 1990s, his name slipped from the headlines as injuries cut into his playing time later in his career. Though they are no longer the prominent stars that they once were, the Hills continue to have an impact on professional sports.

RETIRING FROM FOOTBALL

During his playing years, Calvin had been known as a fierce competitor and one of the NFL's most aggressive rushers. His teammates valued his quiet leadership, as well as his abilities on the field. Although injuries took a toll on his health and he physically reached the point where he could no longer compete at the same level as before, Calvin continued to show the same leadership skills during the final years of his career.

His last game as a professional football player was in 1981, with the Cleveland Browns. When he walked off the field, though, he didn't leave the sport behind. He remained part of the Browns' organization as a special adviser until 1987. Calvin worked with young players, advising them on how to set up their business affairs and conduct themselves off the field.

Calvin's interest in sports extends beyond football. In 1987, he left the Browns to work as an administrator for the Baltimore Orioles, a Major League Baseball team. Calvin stayed with the Orioles until 1994, when he

Calvin Hill speaks with Cowboys owner Jerry Jones during the team's preseason training camp. Calvin went to work for the team's front office as a player's consultant in 1997.

left the team to work as a private consultant. He also joined with other investors in several unsuccessful attempts to purchase professional sports teams, including the Orioles. He served on the board of a number of organizations and corporations, including President Bill Clinton's Presidential Council on Physical Fitness.

Calvin returned to football in 1997, when he was hired by the Dallas Cowboys to serve as a special consultant to young and troubled players. At the time, some of the team's young players were having a tough time adjusting

THE GRANT HILL COLLECTION OF AFRICAN AMERICAN ART

Grant Hill began collecting art shortly after he began his NBA career. Much of his collection focuses on works by African American artists, including Romare Bearden. Deciding to use his collection to inspire young people to envision a career in the arts, Grant turned a portion of his collection into a traveling exhibition. Called "Something All Our Own," the exhibit traveled to seven U.S. cities between 2003 and 2006. To further raise interest and awareness, Grant and Calvin Hill worked together on a book for the exhibit, and Grant offered a $10,000 college scholarship to promising young artists.

to life in professional sports. Several got into trouble with the law. The Cowboys ownership thought that Calvin would help stabilize the team.

By drawing on his own experiences as a player and his earlier consulting work with the Browns, Calvin has been able to reach out to young and troubled football players. He also works with older players who are nearing retirement, helping them make solid plans for when they leave football.

Calvin's speed and scoring ability on the field are still remembered to this day. He has received numerous honors since his retirement. Since he left the team, only four other Cowboys have rushed for 1,000 yards. Calvin is also a member of the Maryland Sports Hall of Fame as one of the state's most successful athletes.

In December 2008, he received the Doak Walker Legends Award. The award, named for Pro Football Hall of Famer Doak Walker, is presented to former college football players whose extraordinary careers on the field have been bolstered by a record of leadership in the community. Through the award, Calvin was recognized once more for his competitive spirit and dedication to service.

In 2008, Calvin Hill was named the Doak Walker Legends Award recipient. He stands at left with University of Iowa running back Shonn Greene, who also was presented with an award.

GRANT HILL ON AND OFF THE COURT

Early in his career at Duke, Grant developed a reputation as an unselfish and mild-mannered player. Although he cared a great deal about winning, he did not place a great value on personal statistics.

When Grant arrived in the NBA in his rookie season, there was a great deal of pressure on him to perform at a high level. Grant's statistics reflected his ability to score, make rebounds and assists, and guard his opponents. He did not dominate any single category, but instead played every aspect of the game well.

Grant Hill's service to the community has included many visits to schools. Here, he poses with an elementary school class and displays his sportsmanship trophy, which is named after NBA great Joe Dumars.

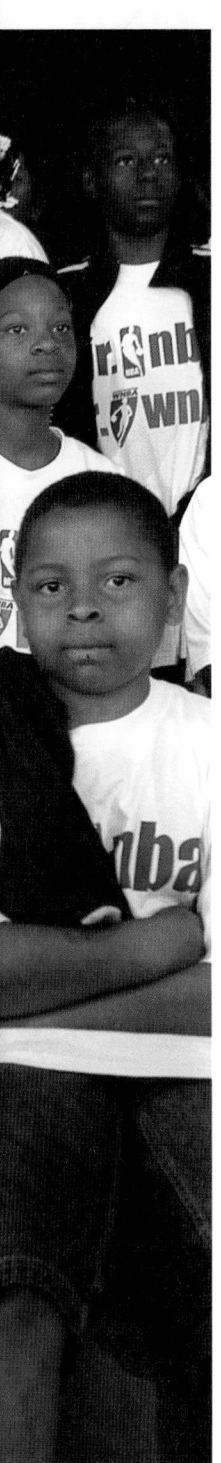

Grant also happened to enter the NBA at a time when the game's biggest superstar, Michael Jordan, was retiring. Fans, and even other players and coaches, saw Grant's skill and athleticism and believed he would take Jordan's place as the NBA's leading scorer. Grant resisted the comparisons to Jordan, arguing that he wanted to be known for playing a well-rounded game.

Grant did, however, become a huge star. His endorsement of Fila athletic shoes helped the company recover from years of slumping sales, while his light-hearted advertisements for the soft drink Sprite ran frequently on TV. Grant became almost as well known for his refined behavior on and off the court as for his skills and endorsements. His soft-spoken manner was a sharp contrast to the sometimes brash behavior of his fellow NBA stars.

Fans confirmed Grant's popularity by voting for him to play in seven All-Star Games. His fellow NBA players have also honored him. After the 2004–2005 and 2007–2008 seasons, Grant received the NBA's Sportsmanship Award for representing the ideals of sportsmanship on the court, including fair play, ethical behavior, and integrity. Grant is the only player to win the award twice since it was first given at the end of the 1995–1996 season.

Grant also remains committed to community service. Throughout his career, he has frequently spoken at local schools, encouraging students to work hard and set goals for themselves. He set up scholarship funds for students in Orlando, Florida, and Detroit, Michigan, and served as the vice chairman of the 1999 Special Olympics. In 1998, Grant paid tribute to his father by donating $100,000 to Duke University to establish the Calvin Hill Scholarship Endowment Fund through Duke's divinity school.

Grant's career-high scoring numbers during the 1998–1999 season were a response to critics who said he couldn't be a

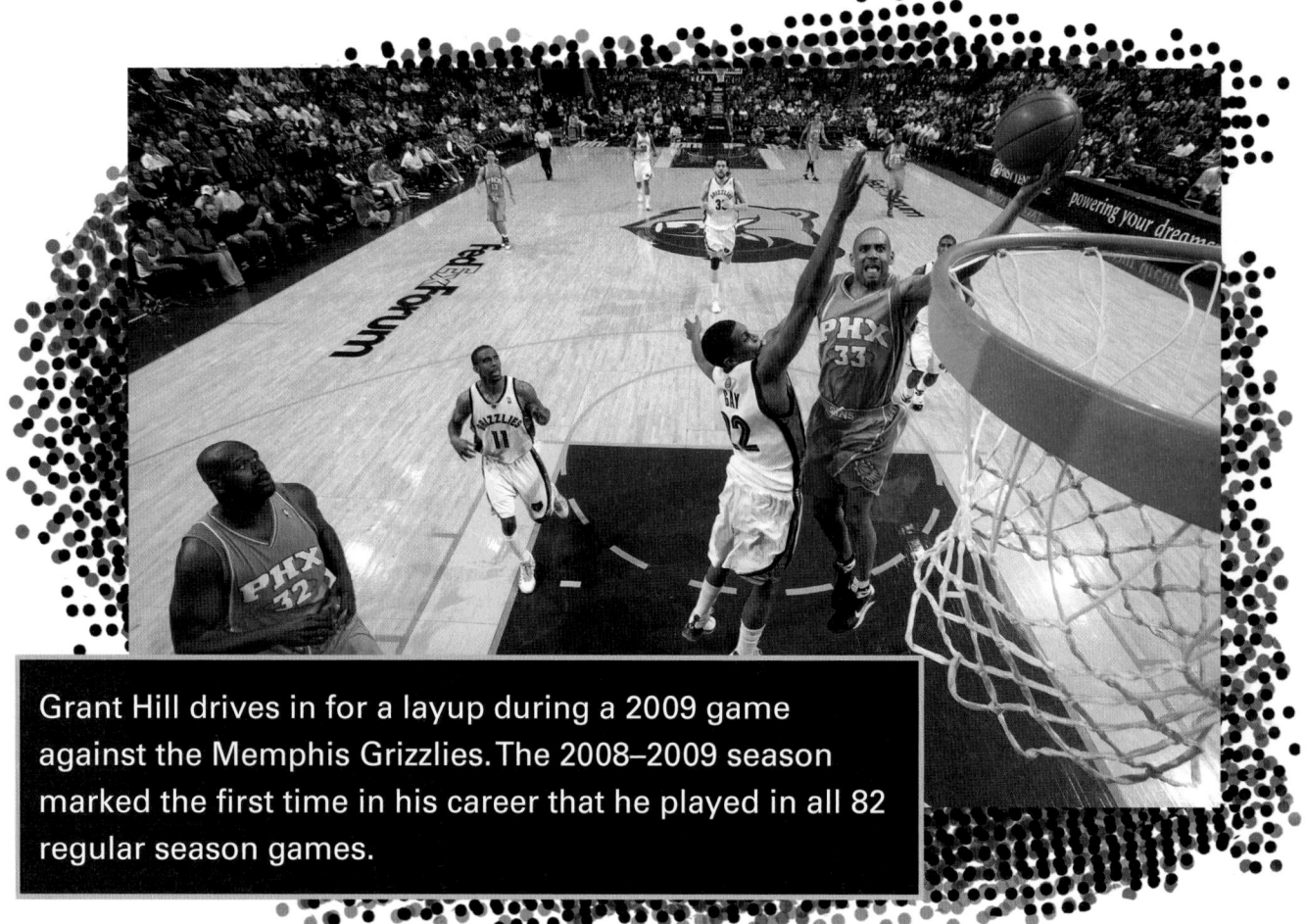

Grant Hill drives in for a layup during a 2009 game against the Memphis Grizzlies. The 2008–2009 season marked the first time in his career that he played in all 82 regular season games.

great scorer. Unfortunately, his career-threatening ankle injury in 1999–2000 was also the result of responding to critics who said he wasn't a tough player when he was first injured. Grant tried to play on the hurt ankle and only made it worse. He also tried to come back from the injury too quickly while he was playing for Orlando. He wanted to justify the big contract that he had signed with the team.

Grant inherited his competitive nature from his father. It has driven him to succeed from the time he first began playing sports. Since his injury, Grant has learned to be more patient. However, he remains a fierce competitor, as shown by his performance during the 2008–2009 season with the Phoenix Suns, when the team battled injuries in an unsuccessful attempt to win a playoff spot.

TIMELINE

1947

Calvin Hill is born in Baltimore, Maryland.

1965

He wins a football and track scholarship to Yale University.

1967

Calvin helps lead Yale to the Ivy League football title with a 9–0 record.

1968

Yale shares the Ivy League title with Harvard, going 8–0–1 for the season. Calvin becomes Yale's all-time leading scorer and is named an All-American player.

1969

Calvin is picked in the first round of the NFL draft by the Dallas Cowboys. He goes on to win the league's Offensive Rookie of the Year Award.

1971

The Dallas Cowboys win their first Super Bowl.

1972

Grant Hill is born in Dallas, Texas.

1974

Calvin plays his final season with Dallas.

1976

The Hills move to Washington, D.C. Calvin starts playing for the Washington Redskins.

1978

Calvin begins playing for the Cleveland Browns.

1981

Calvin retires from playing football.

1985

Grant wins a national tournament with his AAU youth team.

1990

Grant attends Duke University.

1991

Grant helps Duke University win its first NCAA men's basketball championship.

1992

The Duke Blue Devils repeat as NCAA champions.

1994

Grant is named ACC Player of the Year after leading the Blue Devils to another NCAA championship final. He is picked in the first round of the NBA draft by the Detroit Pistons.

1995

Grant leads the NBA in All-Star votes and is named the league's Rookie of the Year.

1996

Grant plays for U.S. men's Olympic basketball team, winning a gold medal.

1999

Grant becomes the second player in NBA history to lead his team in scoring, rebounds, and assists in three seasons.

2000

The Detroit Pistons trade Grant to the Orlando Magic. An ankle injury causes him to miss most of the next four seasons.

2004–2005

Grant plays in his first full season for the Magic. He is named to his seventh All-Star Game.

2007

Grant leaves the Magic to play for the Phoenix Suns.

2008

Grant wins his second NBA Sportsmanship Award.

2009

Grant plays in all 82 games of the 2008–2009 season for the Phoenix Suns; in July, he re-signs with the Suns for two years.

GLOSSARY

assist In sports, the act of enabling another player to make a good play.

divinity school A professional school having a religious curriculum, especially for ministerial candidates.

draft The process by which professional teams select college or amateur players.

endorsement The act of giving support or approval.

Final Four The semifinal round of the NCAA college basketball championship in which four teams compete for the chance to play in the championship game.

fullback An offensive football position often used for blocking.

integrity The quality of having strong moral or artistic values.

Ivy League A league of universities and colleges in the northeastern United States that has a reputation for scholastic achievement and social prestige.

linebacker A defensive football position that takes a position close behind the line of scrimmage.

Pro Bowl The All-Star game of the National Football League.

quarterback The position of a football player in the backfield who directs the team's offense.

rebound The act of grabbing or taking possession of a basketball after a shot is missed.

recruit To enroll or seek to enroll a student at a college; for athletes, often with the enticement of an athletic scholarship.

rookie A first-year participant in a professional sport.

running back In football, an offensive player who tries to advance the ball by carrying on plays from the line of scrimmage.

rushing In football, an attempt to advance the ball by running into the line.

scholarship A form of financial aid awarded to a student for high academic, artistic, or athletic achievement; a scholarship does not have to be paid back.

sportsmanship Fairness in following the rules of a game.

staph infection A type of infection caused by *Staphylococcus* bacteria, which often begins with a cut that gets infected with the bacteria.

steal In basketball, taking control of the ball from a player on the other team.

touchdown In football, a score accomplished by crossing the opponent's goal line with the ball.

tournament A sports competition in which participants play a series of games to determine the winner.

FOR MORE INFORMATION

Amateur Athletic Union (AAU)

1910 Hotel Plaza Road

Lake Buena Vista, FL 32830

(407) 934-7200

Web site: http://image.aausports.org/index.html

The Amateur Athletic Union is an organization that offers amateur sports programs for all people and promotes good sportsmanship and good citizenship.

Atlantic Coast Conference (ACC)

P.O. Drawer ACC

Greensboro, NC 27417-6724

(336) 854-8787

Web site: http://www.theacc.com

The ACC was founded in 1953 in North Carolina and now has 12 university members. The member teams participate in 20 sports, including football and basketball, in the NCAA's Division I.

The Ivy League

Council of Ivy Group Presidents

228 Alexander Street, 2nd Floor

Princeton, NJ 08540

(609) 258-6426

Web site: http://www.ivyleaguesports.com

This organization sponsors conference championships in 33 sports in both men's and women's divisions.

Naismith Memorial Basketball Hall of Fame

1000 West Columbus Avenue

Springfield, MA 01105

(413) 781-6500

Web site: http://hoophall.com

The Basketball Hall of Fame presents all aspects of the game, including the invention and history of the sport.

National Basketball Association (NBA)

Fan Relations

645 Fifth Avenue

New York, NY 10022

(212) 407-8000

Web site: http://www.nba.com

The NBA and its Web site provide information on the history of basketball, the players, the leagues, and the statistics, among other facts.

National Collegiate Athletic Association (NCAA)

700 W. Washington Street

P.O. Box 6222

Indianapolis, IN 46206-6222

(317) 917-6222

Web site: http://www.ncaa.org

The NCAA is a voluntary organization by which U.S. colleges and universities govern their athletics programs. The Web site provides information on programs, schools, players, records, and the history of the NCAA.

National Football Foundation

433 East Las Colinas Boulevard, Suite 1130

Irving, TX 75039

(972) 556-1000

Web site: http://www.footballfoundation.com

The National Football Foundation promotes amateur football by helping to encourage the qualities of leadership, drive for excellence, competitive zeal, and sportsmanship.

National Football League (NFL)

208 Park Avenue

New York, NY 10017

(212) 450-2000

Web site: http://www.nfl.com

The largest professional football league in the United States, the NFL is evenly divided into the American Football Conference (AFC) and the National Football Conference (NFC), with each conference having four divisions with four teams each.

USA Basketball
5465 Mark Dabling Boulevard
Colorado Springs, CO 80918-3842
(719) 590-4800
Web site: http://www.usabasketball.com

This nonprofit organization is the national governing group for both men's and women's basketball in the United States. It is responsible for the selection, training, and fielding of USA teams that compete in the International Basketball Federation's sponsored competitions.

WEB SITES

Due to the changing nature of Internet links, Rosen Publishing has developed an online list of Web sites related to the subject of this book. This site is updated regularly. Please use this link to access the list:

http://www.rosenlinks.com/sfam/hill

FOR FURTHER READING

Brill, Bill, and Mike Krzyzewski. *A Season Is a Lifetime: The Inside Story of the Duke Blue Devils and Their Championship Seasons*. New York, NY: Simon & Schuster, 1993.

Chansky, Art. *Blue Blood: Duke-Carolina: Inside the Most Storied Rivalry in College Hoops*. New York, NY: Thomas Dunne Books, 2005.

Corbett, Bernard M., and Paul Simpson. *The Only Game That Matters: The Harvard/Yale Rivalry*. New York, NY: Crown Publishers, 2004.

Einhorn, Eddie, and Ron Rapoport. *How March Became Madness*. Chicago, IL: Triumph Books, 2006.

Hill, Grant. *Change the Game: One Athlete's Thoughts on Sports, Dreams, and Growing Up*. New York, NY: Warner Books, 1996.

Hill, Grant. *Something All Our Own: The Grant Hill Collection of African American Art*. Durham, NC: Duke University Press, 2004.

Maher, Tom, and Mark Speck. *The World Football League Encyclopedia*. Haworth, NJ: Saint Johann Press, 2006.

Monk, Cody. *Legends of the Dallas Cowboys*. Champaign, IL: Sports Publishing, 2004.

Rappoport, Ken. *Jason Kidd: Leader on the Court*. Berkeley Heights, NJ: Enslow Publishing, 2004.

Roth, John, and Ned Hinshaw. *The Encyclopedia of Duke Basketball*. Durham, NC: Duke University Press, 2006.

Rubin, Sam. *Yale Football*. Chicago, IL: Arcadia Publishing, 2006.

Rud, Jeff. *Steve Nash: The Making of an MVP*. New York, NY: Puffin, 2007.

Sharp, Drew, and Terry Foster. *The Great Detroit Sports Debate*. Champaign, IL: Sports Publishing, 2006.

BIBLIOGRAPHY

Adelman, Ken. "Passing the Ball: Sports Stardom Struck Twice in This Family. Calvin Hill Lived It on the Football Field—Now It's Grant's Turn." *Washingtonian*, April 1997, p. 33.

Branch, Shelly. "All in the Family." *Fortune*, August 4, 1997, p. 76.

Brill, Bill, and Mike Krzyzewski. *A Season Is a Lifetime: The Inside Story of the Duke Blue Devils and Their Championship Seasons*. New York, NY: Simon & Schuster, 1993.

Case, Jeff. "Grant Hill's Art Exhibit Spreads Magic." Newsday.com, December 19, 2003. Retrieved April 15, 2009 (http://www.newsday.com/topic/ocb-arts-granthillinterview,0,993768.story).

Chansky, Art. *Blue Blood: Duke-Carolina: Inside the Most Storied Rivalry in College Hoops*. New York, NY: Thomas Dunne Books, 2005.

Corbett, Bernard M., and Paul Simpson. *The Only Game That Matters: The Harvard/Yale Rivalry*. New York, NY: Crown Publishers, 2004.

Denlinger, Ken. "The Birth of a Rivalry: Passions Loosed in '72 Title Game Ignited 20 Years' War." *Washington Post*, December 13, 1992, p. D01.

Dixon, Oscar. "Calvin Hill Quite Happy to Be 'Grant's Father.'" *USA Today*, December 6, 1994, p. 02C.

Geffner, Michael P. "The Name of the Father." *Sporting News* (Charlotte, NC), January 16, 1995, p. 24.

GrantHill.com. "Hill Pushes Suns Over Jazz." March 26, 2009. Retrieved May 9, 2009 (http://granthill.com/hilltop/?p=47).

Hill, Grant. *Change the Game: One Athlete's Thoughts on Sports, Dreams, and Growing Up*. New York, NY: Warner Books, 1996.

Hopes, Lynn. "Hill's Father Says Son Grant Eager to Resume Career." *Orlando Sentinel*, June 26, 2003, p. D5.

Katz, Michael. "Calvin Hill a Fan Again at 34." *New York Times*, December 12, 1981, Section 1, p. 15.

Mandell, Ted. *Heart Stoppers and Hail Marys: The Greatest College Football Finishes (Since 1970)*. South Bend, IN: Hardwood Press, 2006.

Ryan, Bob. "Granted, He's a Star in the Making." *Boston Globe*, December 1, 1994, p. 79.

Zang, David. "Calvin Hill Interview." *Journal of Sport History*, Winter 1988. Retrieved April 15, 2009 (http://www.la84foundation.org/SportsLibrary/JSH/JSH1988/JSH1503/jsh1503g.pdf).

INDEX

A

All-America teams, 8, 12, 15, 23
All-Star teams, 12, 28, 30, 31, 37
Atlantic Coast Conference, 19, 20, 22

C

Chaney, Don, 28
Change the Game, 19
Chester J. LaRoche Award, 15–16
Cleveland Browns, 27–28, 32, 34

D

Dallas Cowboys, 9, 17, 23, 25–26, 33–34
Detroit Pistons, 22, 28, 30–31
Doak Walker Legends Award, 34
Duke University, 5, 12, 13, 17, 19–22, 35, 37

G

Gentry, Alvin, 31

H

Hill, Calvin
   college career, 5, 13–16
   early years, 6–9
   going pro, 16–17, 23, 25–28
   legacy in sports, 5, 32–34
Hill, Grant
   college career, 5, 13, 17, 19–22
   early years, 6, 9, 11–12
   going pro, 22–23, 28, 30–31
   legacy in sports, 5, 34, 35, 37–38
Hill, Janet, 6, 9, 11, 13

J

Jordan Olivar Award, 16

K

Krzyzewski, Mike, 17, 19

L

Landry, Tom, 17, 25

M

Maryland Sports Hall of Fame, 34

N

National Basketball Association, 5, 22, 23, 28, 30, 32, 34, 35, 37
National Collegiate Athletic Association, 5, 17, 20, 22
National Football League, 5, 16–17, 23, 25, 26, 28, 32

O

Orlando Magic, 30–31, 38

P

Phoenix Suns, 31, 38
Pro Bowl, 25, 26

S

Special Olympics, 37
Super Bowl, 25

W

Washington Redskins, 9, 27
World Football League, 26

Y

Yale University, 5, 8–9, 13–16, 23

ABOUT THE AUTHOR

Jason Porterfield is a journalist and writer who lives in Chicago, Illinois. His numerous books include *Baseball in the American League Central Division*, *Baseball in the National League East Division*, *Basketball in the ACC*, and *Basketball in the Big East*.

PHOTO CREDITS

Designer: Les Kanturek; Editor: Kathy Kuhtz Campbell;
Photo Researcher: Marty Levick